HIS LIGHT SHINES

A Guide to Writing with God

By Amy J Romine

© **2025 Amy J Romine**

All rights reserved. No part of this book may be reproduced, stored in a retrieval system, or transmitted in any form or by any means— electronic, mechanical, photocopy, recording, or otherwise— without the prior written permission of the author, except for brief quotations in reviews or articles.

Published by WritesRomine Books

ISBN: 9 781300 529323

For permissions, inquiries, or more information, contact:

writesromine@gmail.com

hislightshineswriters.blogspot.com

CONTENTS

PART 1: THE SPARK 5

    Chapter 1: The Call to Write 7

    Chapter 2: The Kernel Idea -- Finding Your Story's Heart 10

    Chapter 3: Writing with Faith and Purpose 13

    Chapter 4: Creating Relatable Characters 17

    Chapter 5: Crafting a Compelling Plot 22

    Chapter 6: Worldbuilding with Heart 26

    Chapter 7: The Power of Authentic Voice 30

    Chapter 8: Mastering Dialogue That Feels Real 35

    Chapter 9: The Art of Pacing and Flow 40

    Chapter 10: The Revision Process -- Embracing the Art of Rewriting .. 45

    Chapter 11: Navigating Feedback with Grace and Grit 50

    Chapter 12: Finishing Strong -- Embracing the Final Stretch 54

    Chapter 13: The Truth About Writing -- Finding Your Own Way 58

    Chapter 14: The Foundation of Everything -- Market Research for Writers 63

    Chapter 15: Building Your Author Brand Without Losing Your Soul 67

    Chapter 16: Social Media for Writers -- More Than Just Book Promo. 71

    Chapter 17: Connecting with Readers -- Community Over Sales 75

    Chapter 18: The Balance of Creativity and Marketing 79

    Chapter 19: Writing with God -- The Heartbeat of Your Creative Journey 83

EXTRAS 88

Unleash Your Divine Spark and Write Stories That Matter

Have you ever felt a whisper in your soul urging you to write? A story simmering beneath the surface, waiting to burst into life? In His Light Shines: A Guide to Writing with God, Amy J Romine invites you on a transformative journey where creativity meets faith, and words become a sacred offering.

This isn't just another writing manual—it's a heartfelt companion for Christian writers ready to answer the call. From finding your story's heartbeat to crafting characters that leap off the page, Romine blends practical wisdom with spiritual depth to help you write with purpose and courage. Discover how to weave God's light into every sentence, conquer self-doubt, and build a reader community that resonates with your authentic voice—all while staying true to the One who planted the desire in your heart.

Packed with reflection prompts, prayers, and creative exercises, His Light Shines is your roadmap to storytelling that inspires, heals, and transforms—both your readers and yourself. Whether you're staring at a blank page or buried in a draft, this book will ignite your passion and remind you: your words are holy ground.

Are you ready to write with God and let your light shine?

PART 1: THE SPARK

Introduction: The Call to Write

You're here because something deep inside you feels called to create. Maybe it's been a quiet whisper, a nudge you've felt for years. Or perhaps it's a sudden spark, like a flame igniting your heart with stories waiting to be told. Whatever brought you here, know this: your words matter.

Writing isn't just about filling pages. For the Christian writer, it's a sacred act--an offering. It's a way to reflect God's light in a world that desperately needs hope, truth, and authenticity. Your story has the power to inspire, heal, and transform--not just others, but yourself in the process.

This book is your guide, but more importantly, it's your companion on the journey. You'll learn about the craft, the calling, and the courage it takes to write with purpose. But before we dive into the mechanics, let's pause and acknowledge the One who placed this desire in your heart.

***

Reflection Prompt:

When did you first feel the nudge to write? What stirred your heart to pick up the pen (or open that blank document)?

Prayer:

Heavenly Father, thank You for the gift of creativity. Thank You for the stories You plant within us--stories filled with purpose and light. As I embark on this journey, help me to trust in Your guidance, to write with courage, and to honor You with my words. Amen.

CHAPTER 1:

THE CALL TO WRITE

So, you've felt the nudge to write. Maybe it was a gentle whisper, like a soft breeze stirring the leaves of your heart, or perhaps it hit you like a rogue wave while sipping your morning coffee, nearly knocking your mug out of your hands. Either way, here you are, staring at a blank page, wondering if you're really cut out for this. Let me clear that up for you: You are.

Why We Write (Hint: It's Not Just for the Coffee)

Writing isn't just about stringing words together like beads on a necklace. It's about meaning, connection, and sometimes convincing ourselves that hitting the word count counts as cardio. But beyond the caffeine-fueled sprints and bouts of existential dread, there's a deeper pull--something sacred.

Consider this: "In the beginning, God created..." (Genesis 1:1). The very first thing we know about God is that He created. And guess what? You're made in His image. That creative itch you have? It's not random. It's divine.

Writing is not just an outlet; it's a reflection of the divine spark within you. It's as if God whispered a story into your soul, waiting for you to bring it to life with your words. Even if you think you're just scribbling ideas on napkins or composing notes on your phone at 2 a.m., that, my friend, is holy ground.

The Myths We Believe About Writing

"I need to be inspired 24/7."

Nope. If we waited for inspiration to strike every time, we'd all be staring at blank pages, possibly questioning our life choices. Writing is less about waiting for the muse and more about showing up, even when the muse is on vacation in the Bahamas.

"My story doesn't matter."

Lies. Big, fat, hairy lies. Your story matters because it's yours. It carries your unique fingerprint, perspective, and the lessons God has etched into your life. Imagine if David had thought, "Eh, my life as a shepherd isn't that interesting." We'd miss out on Psalms, and let's be honest, where would our Instagram captions be without them?

"I have to be perfect."

Oh, bless your heart. Perfectionism is just fear wearing a fancy hat. God doesn't call us to perfection; He calls us to faithfulness. Besides, have you ever met a perfect person? Yeah, me neither. And if you think you have, check their Wi-Fi history.

So, What's the Call?

The call to write is less about achieving literary fame and more about obedience. Maybe your words will reach thousands.

Maybe they'll impact just one person. Either way, that's sacred ground.

Writing isn't about impressing people; it's about expressing what God has placed on your heart. It's about showing up, even when the words feel clunky, even when you doubt yourself, even when your cat judges you from across the room.

***

Reflection Prompt:

What keeps you from writing boldly? What would change if you believed your words were part of God's bigger story?

Prayer:

Lord, thank You for the stories within me. Give me the courage to write, not for approval, but as an act of faith. Help me trust that my words matter because they come from You. Amen.

CHAPTER 2:

THE KERNEL IDEA -- FINDING YOUR STORY'S HEART

Picture this: You have an idea. It's shiny, exciting, and you're convinced it'll be the next big thing. Fast forward two weeks, and it's gathering dust in your "Abandoned Drafts" folder, right next to your New Year's resolutions. What happened? You had a spark but no firewood. That's where the kernel idea comes in.

What Is a Kernel Idea?

The kernel idea is the heart of your story--the "why" behind the "what." It's not just a cool plot twist or a quirky character; it's the core truth you're exploring.

Think of it like this:

Plot: A pirate searches for treasure.

Kernel Idea: What if the real treasure isn't gold but redemption?

Your kernel idea is like the Wi-Fi signal for your story. You might not see it, but without it, everything falls apart. It's the thing that keeps your narrative connected, meaningful, and, well, working.

Why It Matters (Beyond Impressing Your Book Club)

Clarity: When you know your kernel idea, you stop chasing every shiny subplot that pops up like a squirrel at a picnic. You stay focused, which is impressive in a world full of distractions (looking at you, TikTok).

Consistency: It keeps your story from feeling like a literary buffet--a little bit of everything but nothing satisfying. Think of it as the main dish; everything else is just the side salad.

Emotional Punch: Readers connect with stories that have a heartbeat. The kernel idea is that heartbeat. Without it, your story is like decaf coffee--technically functional but missing the spark.

How to Find Yours (Without a Treasure Map)

What keeps you up at night?

The questions that haunt you often hold the key to your kernel idea. (No, not "Did I lock the front door?" although that's valid.) More like, "What does forgiveness really look like?" or "Can people truly change?"

What breaks your heart?

Stories rooted in deep emotion resonate because they're real. If something moves you to tears or makes you want to rant passionately at your unsuspecting dog, there's probably a story kernel there.

What truth do you want to explore?

Not preach, but explore. The best stories don't hand out answers; they invite readers to wrestle with questions, like spiritual CrossFit.

Once You've Got It, Now What?

Test Every Scene: Does this support my kernel idea? If not, does it need to be there? Or is it just literary window dressing?

Let It Evolve: Your kernel idea might shift as you write. That's okay. Growth isn't just for characters. Your story can grow, too, like that plant you forgot to water but somehow survived.

Example:

Les Misérables isn't just about a guy running from the law. It's about grace, redemption, and the idea that people can change. It's also about how long Victor Hugo thought was an acceptable word count (spoiler: a lot).

Reflection Prompt:

What's the heartbeat of your story? If you stripped away the plot, what truth would remain?

Prayer:

God, thank You for the ideas You plant in my heart. Help me to see the deeper purpose behind my stories. Guide my words to reflect the truths You've shown me. Amen.

CHAPTER 3:
WRITING WITH FAITH AND PURPOSE

So, you've got the call to write. You've found your kernel idea. Now what? Time to sit down and write with the grace, focus, and efficiency of a caffeinated squirrel, right? Well, not exactly. Writing with faith and purpose isn't about sprinting to the finish line. It's about creating with intention, breathing life into words that not only entertain but also inspire, encourage, and reflect the light of God.

What Does It Mean to Write with Faith?

Writing with faith doesn't mean every story has to be wrapped in Bible verses or feature an angelic choir in the background (although, let's be honest, that could be pretty cool). It means writing from a place of authenticity, rooted in your relationship with God. Faith is the undercurrent, not always the headline.

Think of it like adding salt to a dish. You don't always see it, but you definitely notice when it's missing. Your faith flavors your writing--whether you're penning a heartfelt memoir, crafting a dystopian novel, or even jotting down a grocery list (because let's be real, faith is required to tackle a budget-friendly grocery trip these days).

The Purpose Behind Your Words

Let's face it, writing can feel like shouting into the void, hoping someone, somewhere, hears you. But what if we flipped that perspective? What if your words weren't just filling space but planting seeds?

Your story might be the answer to someone's silent prayer.

Your words could be the encouragement someone needed on their hardest day.

Your characters might be the mirror that helps someone see themselves clearly for the first time.

Writing with purpose isn't about preaching; it's about reaching.

The Struggles Are Real (and Holy)

Let's not romanticize this: writing can be hard. Some days it feels like wrestling with an octopus made of plot holes, dangling participles, and existential dread. But here's the twist: that struggle? It's sacred.

Moses had stage fright. David was an underdog. Jonah literally ran away from his assignment. And yet, God worked through them. If God can use a reluctant prophet and a teenage shepherd, He can definitely use your messy first draft.

How to Write with Faith and Purpose (Without Losing Your Mind)

Start with Prayer, Not Panic: Before you write, pause. Invite God into the process. It doesn't have to be fancy. A simple, "Okay, God, let's do this" works just fine.

Write Like No One's Watching (Because They Aren't Yet): Don't get bogged down trying to impress an imaginary audience. Write the story God put on your heart, not the one you think will trend.

Trust the Process (Even When It's a Hot Mess): Not every writing day will be glorious. Some days you'll write gold. Other days, it'll feel like you're typing with oven mitts on. Show up anyway.

Let Go of the Outcome: Your job is to be faithful to the process, not to control the results. Whether your story reaches one person or a million, its value isn't measured by numbers but by obedience.

A Real-Life Example:

Ever heard of C.S. Lewis? (Of course you have. If not, quick, Google him so we can still be friends.) He didn't set out to create a Christian allegory with The Chronicles of Narnia. He wrote a story about a lion, a wardrobe, and some curious kids... and in doing so, crafted one of the most powerful reflections of faith and redemption in literature. The message wasn't forced; it flowed naturally from who he was and what he believed.

***

Reflection Prompt:

What would your writing look like if you stopped worrying about perfection and simply trusted God with the process?

Prayer:

God, thank You for the stories You've planted in my heart. Help me write with boldness, not for applause, but to honor the gifts You've given me. Teach me to trust the process, embrace the mess, and find joy in the journey. Amen.

CHAPTER 4:
CREATING RELATABLE CHARACTERS

Alright, so you've answered the call to write, discovered your kernel idea, and embraced writing with faith and purpose. But here's the thing: even the most powerful message will fall flat if your characters are about as interesting as a soggy piece of toast. You need characters who leap off the page, tap dance into your readers' hearts, and refuse to leave-- even after the last chapter.

Why Characters Matter More Than Plot Twists (Yes, Really)

Sure, plot twists are fun. Who doesn't love a jaw-dropping revelation that makes you shout, "I did NOT see that coming!" But guess what? If your characters are flat, no one will care. Readers stick around for characters they love (or love to hate).

Think about it:

Would The Lord of the Rings be the same without Frodo and Sam's friendship?

Would Pride and Prejudice still be iconic without Elizabeth Bennet's sass and Mr. Darcy's brooding charm?

Would we cry over a volleyball named Wilson if not for Tom Hanks in Cast Away? (Be honest. You did.)

The Anatomy of a Relatable Character

So, what makes a character memorable? Spoiler alert: it's not about making them perfect. In fact, perfection is boring. (Imagine having a friend who always says and does the right thing. You'd uninvite them from game night real quick.)

Here's what you need:

Flaws:
Yes, flaws. Give them quirks, insecurities, or bad habits. Maybe your hero is afraid of public speaking or eats cereal with orange juice. Whatever it is, flaws make them human.

Goals:

Every character wants something. It could be as big as saving the world or as simple as finding the perfect cup of coffee. Their goal drives the story.

Motivation:

Why do they want what they want? The deeper the motivation, the more your readers will connect.

Conflict:
No one likes a story where everything goes smoothly. (Yawn.) Internal and external conflicts are the spice of life... and of good fiction.

Growth:

Characters should evolve. If they're the same at the end of the story as they were at the beginning, what was the point?

Faith + Flaws = Real Characters

When writing faith-based stories, there's a temptation to create characters who are walking devotionals. Resist that urge. Yes, let their faith influence their actions, but don't shy away from doubt, struggle, and failure. Faith is most compelling when it's real, messy, and hard-won.

Consider Peter in the Bible. He was passionate but impulsive, full of faith one minute and denying Jesus the next. That complexity makes him relatable. Imagine if Peter had been flawless. Yawn. No thanks.

The "Get to Know Your Character" Interview

Want to deepen your characters? Sit them down for an imaginary interview. Ask weird questions. Here are a few to get you started:

What's your biggest fear?

What's your go-to comfort food?

What lie do you believe about yourself?

What would you do if you found a time machine?

How do you react under pressure... like when your Wi-Fi goes down?

Their answers might surprise you--and spark new story ideas.

Common Character Pitfalls (And How to Avoid Them)

The Perfect Protagonist:

They ace every challenge, everyone loves them, and they never make mistakes. Ugh. Give them some struggles, please.

The One-Dimensional Villain:

"I'm evil because... um, reasons." Nope. Even villains think they're the hero of their own story. Give them depth.

The Missing Motivation:

If your character does things "just because," your readers will notice. Always ask: Why?

Real-Life Inspiration

Basing characters on real people? Totally fine. Just tweak the details unless you want awkward family reunions. ("Is Aunt Linda really the villain in your book?" "Oh look, pie!" changes subject)

Better yet, blend traits from multiple people. Take your cousin's sarcasm, your neighbor's obsession with lawn gnomes, and your own fear of commitment to coffee shop punch cards. Boom. Unique character.

Reflection Prompt:

Think of your favorite character from any book or movie. What makes them unforgettable? How can you apply that to your own writing?

Prayer:

God, thank You for the beauty and complexity of people. Help me create characters that reflect both the struggles and the hope of real life. Teach me to write with authenticity, grace, and a deep understanding of the hearts You've crafted. Amen.

CHAPTER 5:
CRAFTING A COMPELLING PLOT

Okay, so you've got your relatable characters who are bursting with quirks, dreams, and just the right amount of existential angst. Now what? You can't have them sitting around sipping coffee and exchanging witty banter for 300 pages (unless you're aiming for the most niche novel ever). They need a plot--the thing that makes your readers say, "Just one more chapter..." at 2 a.m.

What Is a Plot Anyway? (It's More Than Stuff Happening)

A plot isn't just a sequence of events. It's a structured journey where your characters face challenges, make decisions, and (hopefully) grow. Imagine your plot as the skeleton of your story. Without it, your narrative is basically jelly. Wobbly. Unstable. Not good.

Here's the basic plot recipe:

Introduction: Meet the characters. Set the scene. Life is normal. (But not for long!)

Inciting Incident: Boom! Something disrupts the status quo. The character can't unsee it.

Rising Action: Challenges, conflicts, and complications. Basically, things get messy.

Climax: The big showdown. The moment everything has been building toward.

Falling Action: The dust settles. Characters deal with the aftermath.

Resolution: Tying up loose ends. The story comes full circle.

The Secret Sauce: Conflict

Without conflict, there is no plot. Period. Conflict doesn't have to be explosions or dramatic betrayals (though those are fun). It can be internal, external, or both.

Internal Conflict: The struggle within. Think Frodo battling the ring's influence.

External Conflict: The struggle with outside forces. Think Katniss against the Capitol.

Relational Conflict: Tension between characters. Think Elizabeth Bennet and Mr. Darcy's epic misunderstandings.

If your story feels flat, add conflict. Stir well.

Plotting with Faith (No, Not Blind Faith)

As a faith-driven writer, your plot can reflect spiritual truths without turning into a sermon disguised as fiction. Think parables: simple stories with deeper meanings.

Ask yourself:

What does my character believe at the start?

How will their journey challenge those beliefs?

What truth will they discover by the end?

Growth isn't just for your personal development books. Your characters need it too.

Common Plot Pitfalls (And How to Dodge Them)

The Wandering Plot:

If your story meanders like a lost tourist, tighten it up. Every scene should serve a purpose.

The Predictable Plot:

Plot twists are fun because they surprise us. If readers can guess your twist from page three, you might need to shake things up.

The Overly Complicated Plot:

Plot twists are great. Plot pretzels? Not so much. Don't twist your story into something even you can't follow.

Plotting Techniques (Because Pantsing Is Only Fun Until It's Not)

The Three-Act Structure: Classic. Reliable. Like the little black dress of plotting.

The Hero's Journey: Perfect for epic tales. (Thanks, Joseph Campbell.)

The Snowflake Method: Start small. Expand gradually. Great if you like to build layer by layer.

Find what works for you. There's no "one right way" to plot--unless you're trying to assemble IKEA furniture, and even then, it's debatable.

Keep the Tension Alive (Without Exhausting Your Reader)

Tension isn't just about car chases. It's the feeling of "What will happen next?" You create it through:

Unanswered questions: Leave your reader curious.

High stakes: What does the character stand to lose?

Character dilemmas: Make them choose between two tough options. (Sorry, characters. It's for your growth.)

Reflection Prompt:

What's the central conflict in your story? How does it challenge your characters, and what truth does it reveal?

Prayer:

God, thank You for the gift of story. Help me craft plots that not only entertain but also inspire and reflect Your truth. Teach me to embrace both the twists and the turns, trusting that every part of the journey has purpose. Amen.

CHAPTER 6:

WORLDBUILDING WITH HEART

Alright, buckle up because we're about to dive into worldbuilding--the part of writing where you get to play God. No pressure, right? Whether your story is set in a quaint small town where everyone knows the local baker's cat by name, or on a distant planet where gravity is optional and people communicate through interpretive dance, worldbuilding matters.

Why Worldbuilding Isn't Just for Fantasy Nerds (Though We Love Them)

You might think worldbuilding is only for epic fantasy writers crafting elaborate maps and inventing languages. But here's the truth: every story requires worldbuilding. Whether your characters are battling dragons or battling traffic on the way to a coffee shop, the world they live in shapes who they are and how the story unfolds.

Your story's setting isn't just a backdrop; it's an active participant in the plot. Think of it as the silent character that adds depth, conflict, and flavor to every scene.

The Building Blocks of a Believable World

Location, Location, Location:

Where does your story take place? A bustling city? A sleepy town? A hidden kingdom under the sea? Describe the sights, sounds, and smells. Yes, smells matter. (Ever walked into a room and instantly regretted it? Exactly.)

Culture and Customs:

What do people value? What are their traditions? Do they have quirky sayings like, "Bless your heart," which, depending on context, can be either sweet or shady?

Rules of the World:

Even in fictional worlds, things need to make sense. If magic exists, how does it work? If it's a dystopian future, what went wrong? Consistency is key unless you're aiming for confusion as a plot device.

Weather and Climate:

Does it snow? Rain? Are there two suns? Weather can set the mood, create conflict, or even mirror a character's emotional state. Think of it as atmospheric seasoning.

Faith in the Fabric of Your World

When weaving faith into your world, subtlety often speaks louder than sermons. Instead of a character delivering a three-page monologue on the virtues of grace, show how grace is lived out in the world you've created.

Consider these questions:

What do people believe in your world? (Faith systems, moral codes, personal convictions)

How do those beliefs influence laws, art, relationships, and conflicts?

Is there a sacred space? A ritual? A tradition that reflects deeper truths?

Faith doesn't have to be front and center to be powerful. Sometimes, it's the undercurrent that shapes everything else.

Common Worldbuilding Pitfalls (And How to Avoid Them)

Info-Dumping:

Resist the urge to explain every detail in one giant paragraph. Sprinkle world details naturally through dialogue, action, and character observations.

Inconsistency:

If you say your desert planet has no water, don't have characters sipping lemonade without explaining where the lemons came from.

Generic Settings:

"Small town" isn't enough. What makes this small town unique? Maybe it's the annual "Bake-Off Battle Royale" where things get oddly competitive.

Worldbuilding Hacks for the Busy Writer

The Five Senses Test:

For any scene, ask: What can the character see, hear, smell, taste, and feel? Engaging the senses makes the world come alive.

The "What If" Game:

What if gravity was 10% stronger? What if coffee was outlawed? (Now there's a dystopian novel waiting to happen.)

Map It Out (Literally):

Draw a map. It doesn't have to be fancy--just enough to keep track of where things are. Even if it looks like your dog sketched it, it helps.

Worldbuilding Through Character Eyes

Your world feels most real when experienced through your characters. How does the setting affect them emotionally? Are they comfortable or out of place? Do they roll their eyes at the town's odd traditions, or do they cherish them?

Let the world shape your characters, and let your characters reveal the world.

Reflection Prompt:

What makes your story's setting unique? How does it influence your characters, plot, and themes?

Prayer:

God, thank You for the beauty and diversity of creation. Help me build worlds that reflect both the wonder and the complexity of life. Teach me to weave truth, hope, and purpose into the fabric of my story's setting. Amen.

CHAPTER 7:

THE POWER OF AUTHENTIC VOICE

Ah, voice--that elusive, magical thing writers are always talking about. "Find your voice," they say, as if it's hiding under the couch cushions with the TV remote and three stale Cheerios. But what exactly is voice? And more importantly, how do you find yours without sounding like a knock-off version of your favorite author?

What Is Voice? (Hint: It's Not Just About Being Quirky)

Voice is the unique fingerprint of your writing. It's not just what you say, but how you say it. It's the rhythm of your sentences, the words you choose, the way you paint a picture with language. Think of it like this:

Tone: The mood of your writing. Is it snarky? Serious? Thoughtful? (If you're here, we're guessing you enjoy a dash of snark.)

Style: Your sentence structure, vocabulary, and pacing. Are you concise and punchy or lyrical and poetic?

Perspective: Your worldview seeping through the cracks, intentionally or not. Your experiences, beliefs, and quirks all influence your voice.

Why Voice Matters (A Lot More Than Perfect Grammar)

Great stories aren't just about plot and characters; they're about how those elements are delivered. Two writers could tell the same story, and it would feel completely different because of their voices. That's the magic.

Consider:

J.K. Rowling: Witty, whimsical, and brimming with British charm.

C.S. Lewis: Intellectual, philosophical, with a sprinkle of dry humor.

Dr. Seuss: Rhyming wizard with a knack for making up words that somehow make perfect sense.

Your voice is what keeps readers turning the pages--even if the plot takes a detour (which happens to the best of us).

How to Find Your Authentic Voice (Without Losing Your Mind)

Write Like You Talk (But Edited):

Imagine telling your story to a friend. Not the formal, polished version you'd submit to an English teacher--the real, animated version where your hands flail for emphasis. Start there, then clean it up just enough to make sense on paper.

Stop Trying to Sound "Writerly":

You don't need to use fancy words like "plethora" when "a lot" will do. (Unless "plethora" is your jam, then go for it.) Authenticity beats pretension every time.

Read Widely, Write Often:

Exposure to different voices helps you recognize what resonates with you. Then write. A lot. Your voice will emerge through practice, like a muscle getting stronger with each workout.

Embrace Your Quirks:

Do you love weird metaphors? Use them. Have a dry sense of humor? Let it shine. Your quirks are part of your voice, not something to edit out.

The Role of Faith in Your Voice

Your faith isn't just a theme in your stories; it shapes your voice. Whether you write overtly Christian fiction or stories where faith is a subtle undercurrent, your worldview influences how you see the world--and how you describe it.

Consider:

How does your faith shape your perspective on hope, struggle, and redemption?

Does grace show up in how your characters grow, even if you never use the word "grace"?

Are you writing from a place of authenticity, even when it means confronting hard truths?

Authentic voice comes from honesty, and faith adds depth to that honesty.

Common Voice Pitfalls (And How to Avoid Them)

Mimicking Other Writers:

It's okay to be inspired, but don't copy. The world doesn't need another Tolkien. It needs you.

Overthinking Every Sentence:

Analysis paralysis is real. Write first, edit later. Let your voice flow naturally without critiquing every word as it lands.

Inconsistent Tone:

If your story starts light-hearted and suddenly shifts to dark and brooding with no warning, readers will get whiplash. (Unless that's the point--then carry on.)

Exercises to Strengthen Your Voice

Stream of Consciousness: Write nonstop for five minutes without editing. Let your natural voice take the wheel.

Imitate, Then Innovate: Write a paragraph imitating your favorite author's style. Then rewrite it in your own voice.

Dialogue Challenge: Write a conversation between two characters using only dialogue. No descriptions, no tags. Can you convey their personalities through voice alone?

Reflection Prompt:

What makes your writing sound uniquely "you"? How can you lean into that authenticity instead of hiding it?

Prayer:

God, thank You for the unique voice You've given me. Help me write with honesty, courage, and joy. Teach me to embrace my story, my quirks, and my perspective as gifts from You. Amen.

CHAPTER 8:
MASTERING DIALOGUE THAT FEELS REAL

Alright, writers, let's talk about... talking. Specifically, the art of dialogue. Because nothing pulls a reader out of a story faster than characters who speak like robots trying to sell you life insurance. You know the kind:

"Hello, Jessica. How are you this fine morning?" "I am well, John. Thank you for asking. The weather is pleasant today."

Yawn. Did you fall asleep? I almost did.

Why Dialogue Matters (Spoiler: It's Not Just to Fill Pages)

Dialogue isn't just about characters exchanging words. It's about revealing who they are, advancing the plot, and creating tension. Think of dialogue as the spice in your story stew-- without it, everything tastes bland.

Great dialogue should:

Sound natural, like something a real person would say (but slightly snappier).

Reveal character, showing personality, background, and emotions.

Move the plot forward, not just fill space with idle chatter.

Create tension, because even friendly conversations can have an undercurrent of conflict.

The Secret Sauce of Great Dialogue

Less Is More:

Real people ramble, but your characters shouldn't. Cut the filler. If it doesn't reveal something new or move the story along, it's probably unnecessary.

Subtext Is Everything:

People rarely say exactly what they mean. (Just ask anyone in a group chat.) The tension between what's said and what's meant is where the magic happens.

Example:

"I'm fine." (Translation: I'm absolutely not fine, but please notice and ask again.)

Different Voices for Different Characters:

Your characters should sound distinct. If I covered the names, could I still tell who's speaking? Give them unique speech patterns, slang, or quirks.

Interruptions and Incomplete Thoughts:

People don't talk in perfect sentences. They interrupt, trail off, change topics mid-thought. Use that to make your dialogue feel real.

Faith in Dialogue (Without Preaching at Your Readers)

If your story includes faith elements, dialogue is a powerful way to show belief in action. But here's the key: show, don't sermon.

Instead of:

*"Let me tell you about the four spiritual laws..."

Try:

*"I don't have all the answers, but I know grace isn't something you earn. I learned that the hard way."

See the difference? It feels authentic because it comes from the character's heart, not an invisible megaphone.

Common Dialogue Mistakes (And How to Fix Them)

The Infodump:

"As you know, Karen, we've been best friends since kindergarten, and your love for collecting rare stamps has always been impressive."

Solution: If both characters know it, don't say it. Find a more natural way to slip in the info.

Everyone Sounds the Same:

Make sure your 80-year-old grandma character doesn't talk like your 17-year-old skater dude... unless that's part of the plot twist.

Overusing Names:

"John, pass the salt. Thanks, John. You know, John, this reminds me of our trip to Johnsville."

We get it. His name is John. Relax.

Dialogue Hacks for the Win

Read It Out Loud:

If it sounds awkward out loud, it'll read awkward on the page. Bonus: dramatic readings for your pets.

Eavesdrop Like a Pro:

Listen to real conversations in coffee shops (discreetly, of course). Notice how people speak in fragments, overlap, and leave things unsaid.

Script It:

Write dialogue like a screenplay first--no descriptions, just the back-and-forth. This helps you focus on flow and pacing.

Bonus Tip: Use Silence

Sometimes, what's not said speaks louder. A character's silence in response to a question can be more powerful than a monologue. (Ask any parent who's received a suspiciously quiet toddler in response to, "What are you up to?")

Reflection Prompt:

What does your character's dialogue reveal about them? Are they saying what they mean, or hiding behind words?

Prayer:

God, thank You for the gift of language. Help me write dialogue that feels real, reveals truth, and reflects the depth of human connection. Teach me to listen as much as I write, finding inspiration in the words and silences around me. Amen.

CHAPTER 9:

THE ART OF PACING AND FLOW

Welcome to Chapter 9, where we talk about the unsung hero of storytelling: pacing. It's that subtle force that keeps readers glued to the pages or, alternatively, flipping to see how many pages are left (never a good sign). Think of pacing like music: too slow, and people fall asleep; too fast, and it feels like you're being chased by a caffeinated squirrel. The goal? A rhythm that feels just right.

What Is Pacing (and Why Should You Care)?

Pacing is the speed at which your story unfolds. It's the tempo of your narrative, the rise and fall of action, dialogue, and reflection. Good pacing keeps readers engaged, allowing them to savor emotional moments and race through thrilling scenes without tripping over clunky transitions.

Imagine watching an action movie where every scene is a car chase. Sounds exciting, right? Until you realize that after the tenth explosion, you're just waiting for someone to stop and grab a sandwich. The same goes for your story. Variety is the spice of pacing.

The Two Types of Pacing You Need to Master

Macro Pacing (Big Picture):

This is the overall flow of your story--how quickly the plot moves from beginning to end. It includes:

The inciting incident

Rising tension

Climax

Resolution

Micro Pacing (Scene Level):

This focuses on the pacing within individual scenes. Are your action scenes punchy and fast? Are your emotional moments given room to breathe?

How to Control Pacing Like a Pro

Sentence Length Matters:

Short sentences = fast pace.

Long, descriptive sentences with lots of detail = slower pace, allowing the reader to linger in the moment.

Example:

Fast: She ran. Heart pounding. Breath sharp. Shadows closing in.

Slow: The golden sunset bled across the horizon, casting long shadows that stretched like fingers, lazily caressing the edges of rooftops and quiet streets.

Paragraph Breaks Are Your Friends:

White space on a page speeds things up. Long blocks of text slow things down. Use this strategically to control the reader's experience.

Action vs. Reflection:

Balance is key. Too much action, and your readers don't have time to process. Too much introspection, and they might wander off to reorganize their sock drawer.

Dialogue as a Pacing Tool:

Snappy dialogue can quicken the pace, while longer monologues slow it down. Mix it up depending on the mood of the scene.

Common Pacing Pitfalls (and How to Avoid Them)

The Dreaded Middle Slump:

This is where stories go to die if you're not careful. Inject conflict, raise stakes, or add a twist to keep things moving.

Over-Explaining:
Trust your reader. If you've already shown us your character is sad, you don't need three paragraphs about the symbolism of the wilting houseplant.

Rushed Endings:

Don't sprint to the finish line just because you're eager to type "The End." Give your resolution the attention it deserves.

Faith and Pacing (Because Even Spiritual Growth Has a Rhythm)

Just like in life, spiritual growth in stories isn't linear. Characters might have moments of rapid transformation followed by seasons of doubt or reflection. This ebb and flow mirrors real faith journeys and adds authenticity to your narrative.

Consider:

Are your characters learning lessons too quickly, making their growth feel unearned?

Do they have space to wrestle with their doubts, or are you rushing to the redemption scene?

Tips to Check Your Pacing

Read Your Story Aloud: You'll hear if something drags or feels rushed.

Chapter Check: Does each chapter end with a hook or question that makes the reader want to continue?

Beta Readers: Ask them where they got bored or felt overwhelmed.

Reflection Prompt:

Think about your favorite book or movie. Where did it grip you, and where (if at all) did it lose you? How can you apply those observations to your own writing?

Prayer:

God, thank You for the rhythms of life and story. Help me find the right pace for my words, creating space for both excitement and reflection. Teach me to trust the process, knowing that every pause and every rush serves a purpose. Amen.

CHAPTER 10:

THE REVISION PROCESS -- EMBRACING THE ART OF REWRITING

Welcome to Chapter 10, also known as "The Part Where You Realize Writing Is Actually Rewriting." I know, I know. You thought typing "The End" was the finish line. But plot twist: it's just the beginning.

Why Revision Is Where the Magic Happens

First drafts are like rough sketches--full of potential but often messy, awkward, and held together with metaphorical duct tape. Revision is where you chisel away the excess, polish the gems, and occasionally scream into a pillow because you realize that scene you loved? Yeah, it needs to go.

But here's the thing: revision isn't about fixing mistakes. It's about discovering the heart of your story and making it shine.

Think of it as sculpting. The raw material is there; now you shape it.

The Stages of Revision (Because One Pass Is Never Enough)

Let It Rest:

Before you dive back in, take a break. Step away for a few days (or weeks). This helps you return with fresh eyes, ready to spot things you missed.

Big Picture Edits (Macro Revision):

Does the plot make sense?

Are the character arcs satisfying?

Is the pacing balanced?

Does the story stay true to your kernel idea?

Focus on structure first. Don't sweat the typos yet. It's like redecorating a room--you wouldn't hang pictures before fixing the walls.

Scene-Level Edits:

Does each scene have a purpose?

Is there tension or conflict?

Are character motivations clear?

Trim the scenes that drag, expand the ones that need more depth, and make sure every scene earns its place.

Line Edits (Polishing):

Now we get nitpicky. Sentence structure, word choice, dialogue flow. This is where you swap "very tired" for "exhausted" and delete unnecessary filler words (looking at you, "really" and "just").

Proofreading (The Final Sweep):

Grammar, punctuation, typos. This is the stage where you catch the rogue comma or that sneaky character whose eye color magically changed halfway through the book.

How to Approach Revision Without Losing Your Mind

Don't Edit While You Write:

First drafts are for getting the story down. Revising mid-draft is like trying to fix a flat tire while driving. Finish the draft. Then revise.

Kill Your Darlings (Gently):

Yes, it's painful to cut that witty line or beautifully crafted paragraph. But if it doesn't serve the story, it needs to go. Save it in a "Maybe Later" file if it helps.

Read It Aloud:

Your brain skips over mistakes when reading silently. Reading aloud forces you to hear the rhythm and catch awkward phrasing.

Color-Code Your Draft:

Highlight different elements (dialogue, description, action) to see if you have a good balance. If your page is glowing neon pink with dialogue and no yellow for description, it might be time to add more detail.

Get Feedback (But Not from Your Mom Unless She's Ruthless):
Beta readers, critique partners, or a writing group can offer fresh perspectives. Be open to constructive criticism, but trust your instincts too.

Faith in the Revision Process (Because It's Spiritual Growth in Disguise)

Revision mirrors our own journeys of faith. It's about refining, learning, and growing. Just as we're works in progress, so are our stories.

Grace for Yourself: You won't get it perfect on the first try. Or the second. That's okay.

Trust the Process: Even when it feels messy, each draft brings you closer to the heart of your story.

Pray Through It: When stuck, ask God for clarity. Sometimes the words flow; sometimes you wrestle them out. Both are holy work.

Common Revision Mistakes (And How to Avoid Them)

Fixing Grammar Before Story:

Don't waste time perfecting sentences you might cut later.

Ignoring Feedback:

If multiple people point out the same issue, consider it. (Unless it's just your uncle suggesting more explosions. Then maybe not.)

Over-Editing:

Yes, you can revise too much. At some point, you're not improving--just rearranging furniture. Know when to stop.

Reflection Prompt:

What part of revision feels hardest for you? How can you shift your mindset to see it as part of the creative process, not just a chore?

Prayer:

God, thank You for the gift of revision--for the chance to refine, reshape, and discover deeper truths in my words. Grant me patience, clarity, and courage to let go of what doesn't serve the story. Teach me to embrace the process, knowing that growth happens in the rewriting. Amen.

CHAPTER 11:

NAVIGATING FEEDBACK WITH GRACE AND GRIT

Welcome to Chapter 11, where we tackle the part of writing that can be both incredibly enlightening and, let's be honest, slightly terrifying: receiving feedback. You've poured your heart onto the page, crafted characters you'd protect in a zombie apocalypse, and revised until your coffee mug begged for mercy. Now it's time to let someone else read your masterpiece. Gulp.

Why Feedback Feels Personal (Because It Is... Sort of)

Here's the thing: writing is personal. You're sharing pieces of your heart, your imagination, and possibly your unfiltered opinions on whether pineapple belongs on pizza (a debate for another day). So, when someone critiques your work, it can feel like they're critiquing you.

But here's the truth bomb: feedback is about the work, not your worth. It's a tool, not a judgment. Even the most seasoned authors need editors, beta readers, and critique partners. Feedback isn't a sign of failure; it's a step toward growth.

The Two Types of Feedback (and How to Handle Both)

Constructive Feedback:

This is the gold standard. It points out strengths and areas for improvement, often with specific suggestions. It might sting a little, but it's meant to help you grow.

Example:

"Your dialogue is strong, but consider tightening the pacing in Chapter 3. The tension drops when the characters discuss sandwich toppings for three pages."

Unhelpful Feedback:

Vague, overly harsh, or dismissive comments fall into this category. Sometimes it's more about the critic than your work.

Example:

"I just didn't like it." (Cool. Care to elaborate?)

How to Receive Feedback Without Curling Into a Ball

Pause Before Reacting:

Your first instinct might be to defend your work or declare, "They just don't get it!" Take a breath. Sit with the feedback before responding.

Separate Yourself from Your Work:

You are not your manuscript. Criticism of your story isn't a critique of your value as a person or writer.

Look for Patterns:

If multiple people mention the same issue, it's worth addressing. One person's opinion is subjective; consistent feedback highlights areas for growth.

Ask Clarifying Questions:

If something isn't clear, don't be afraid to ask, "Can you elaborate on what felt flat about this scene?" Specifics help.

Keep What Serves, Discard What Doesn't:

Not all feedback is helpful. Trust your instincts. If a suggestion doesn't align with your vision, it's okay to let it go.

Giving Feedback (Without Crushing Souls)

If you're part of a critique group, remember that giving feedback is an art, too. Aim to be kind, specific, and constructive.

Start with Positives: What worked well?

Be Specific: Instead of "This part was confusing," say, "I wasn't sure why the character suddenly changed their mind here."

End with Encouragement: Highlight potential and growth.

Faith and Feedback (Because It's Not Just About Writing)

Receiving feedback gracefully is a spiritual practice. It teaches humility, patience, and discernment.

Pray for an Open Heart: Before reading critiques, ask God to help you receive feedback with wisdom, not defensiveness.

Anchor Your Identity in Christ: Your worth isn't defined by praise or criticism. You're more than your word count.

Grow Through the Process: Just as faith grows through challenge, your writing strengthens through revision.

Common Feedback Fears (and How to Conquer Them)

"What if they hate it?"

They might. And that's okay. Not every story is for everyone. Focus on finding readers who understand your genre and style.

"What if I can't fix it?"

You can. Writing is a skill, not magic. Every draft is an opportunity to learn.

"What if I lose my voice?"

Feedback should refine your voice, not erase it. Stay true to your vision while being open to improvement.

Reflection Prompt:

How do you respond to feedback? What helps you process critique in a healthy, productive way?

Prayer:

God, thank You for the gift of growth. Help me receive feedback with humility, courage, and grace. Teach me to listen with an open heart, discern what serves my work, and trust in the process. Amen.

CHAPTER 12:

FINISHING STRONG -- EMBRACING THE FINAL STRETCH

You've made it to Chapter 12. Take a moment. Breathe it in. This is the part where we talk about finishing your manuscript without curling into a blanket burrito and questioning all your life choices. You're almost there, and yes, you absolutely can cross that finish line with style, grace, and maybe a celebratory donut (or three).

The Myth of "I'll Never Be Done"

Here's the secret: no book ever feels completely done. Even bestselling authors look at their published books and think, "I could've tweaked that scene..." But perfection isn't the goal. Progress is.

Finishing isn't about tying everything into a perfect bow. It's about knowing when you've told the story you were meant to tell and being brave enough to say, "This is it."

The Final Push (A.K.A. "Keep Going, You've Got This!")

Revisit Your "Why":

Why did you start this story? What message did you want to share? Reconnecting with your purpose can reignite your motivation.

Set Mini Goals:

Break it down. Instead of thinking, "I have 20,000 words left," think, "Today, I'll write 500 words." Small steps lead to big wins.

Create a Ritual:

Light a candle, play a specific playlist, or wear your lucky socks. Whatever helps you get into the zone, do it. Rituals can trick your brain into focus mode.

Embrace the Mess:

The final draft isn't about being flawless. It's about capturing the heart of your story. Perfection is overrated. Authenticity wins.

Visualize "The End":

Picture it. You, typing those glorious words. Maybe there's dramatic background music. Maybe there's confetti (real or imagined). Visualizing success can help you push through the hard parts.

The Emotional Rollercoaster of Finishing

Excitement: "I'm almost done! This is amazing!"

Doubt: "Wait, is this even good?"

Panic: "What if no one likes it?"

Relief: "I DID IT."

Existential Crisis: "Now what?"

All of this is normal. Feel your feelings. Then keep writing.

Faith in the Final Stretch

Finishing a book is like running a race. There's exhilaration and exhaustion, doubt and determination. But here's the thing: God isn't just waiting at the finish line. He's with you every step of the way.

Pray Through the Process: When you're stuck, frustrated, or overwhelmed, pause and pray. Invite God into your writing space.

Trust the Journey: Even if your story doesn't turn out exactly as planned, trust that it's unfolding the way it should.

Celebrate Your Progress: Every word, every chapter, every revision is a victory.

What Comes After "The End"?

Rest: You've earned it. Step away from your manuscript, even if just for a day.

Reflect: What did you learn about yourself through this process?

Revise (Again): Yep, revision still exists. But now you have a complete draft to work with, and that's worth celebrating.

Share Your Work: Whether it's with a trusted friend, a critique group, or an agent, be bold. Your words matter.

Reflection Prompt:

What has this writing journey taught you about persistence, creativity, and faith? How will you carry these lessons into your next project?

Prayer:

God, thank You for the courage to write, the perseverance to finish, and the grace to grow through this journey. Help me trust that my words have purpose and that every story I tell reflects a part of Your greater story. Amen.

CHAPTER 13:

THE TRUTH ABOUT WRITING -- FINDING YOUR OWN WAY

Let's get one thing straight: writing is not for the faint of heart. It's not for the whimsical dreamers who think inspiration floats down like fairy dust or for those who believe there's one magical formula to follow. Writing is gritty, messy, glorious work. It's part art, part discipline, and entirely personal.

The Myth of "The Right Way"

You've probably heard it all:

"You must write every day."

"Outline first or risk chaos."

"Real writers drink black coffee and live in dusty attics."

Spoiler alert: there is no one right way to write. What works for me might not work for you. What works for Jane might be a disaster for John. Writing is like finding the perfect pair of jeans--what fits one person perfectly might make someone else feel like a stuffed sausage. The key is finding what fits you.

Why No One Can Truly Teach You How to Write

1. Writing Is a Personal, Unique Experience.

Writing isn't just a skill; it's an extension of how your brain and heart process the world. It's your lens, your rhythm, your voice. Sure, people can teach you grammar, structure, and techniques. But the act of writing? That's all you.

Your job is to refine your tool--to find the best way to translate the vivid images, emotions, and ideas in your head onto the page. And guess what? That process will be different every time you sit down to write. That's the beauty of it.

2. Writing Styles Are Like Fingerprints--No Two Are Alike.

For me, writing is an all-the-time thing. I can't turn it off. My brain is constantly narrating life, crafting dialogue in line at the grocery store, and mentally editing everything from billboards to text messages.

But for Jane? Maybe she writes best in focused, scheduled sessions with a mug of tea and complete silence. If I tried to copy her process, I'd probably end up frustrated and wondering why my muse ghosted me.

Bottom line: Find out what works for you. That's the real secret.

The Joy of Meeting Other Writers

One of my absolute favorite things is meeting other writers and learning about their unique processes. There's something magical about hearing how someone else approaches their craft--what sparks their creativity, what routines ground them, and even what quirky habits they swear by. Sometimes, I've had the privilege of offering suggestions, little adjustments that helped unlock new pathways for their writing. Watching another writer flourish is one of the most rewarding experiences.

Writing is often tied deeply to emotion. For better or worse, if you're serious about writing, you're emotionally attached to your work--and you should be. That emotional connection fuels your passion, but it also means you need to be mindful of how you manage it. Be conscious of your emotional state when deciding what and when to write. Some days, pouring your heart onto the page feels therapeutic. Other days, it might feel like trying to squeeze water from a stone.

For me, I've found a rhythm that works. I focus on blog posts and social media content during the day--that's when my brain is fresh and can handle the more structured, outward-facing work. Fiction, though? That's my nighttime magic. When the world quiets down, my imagination wakes up. That's how my schedule flows as both a person and a writer. But again, that's my process. Yours might look completely different, and that's not just okay--it's beautiful.

Activities to Discover Your Writing Style

So, how do you figure out what kind of writer you are? Here are some activities to help you explore:

Write at Different Times of Day:

Are you a morning person who thrives with fresh coffee and sunrise vibes? Or do your best ideas hit at 2 a.m. when the world is quiet? Experiment and see.

Change Your Environment:

Try writing in a cozy corner, a noisy cafe, or outside in nature. Pay attention to how each setting affects your focus and creativity.

Experiment with Genres:

Maybe you think you're a fiction writer, but what if your heart sings when you write poetry or memoir? Don't box yourself in too soon.

Play with Word Count Goals:

Some writers love daily word count targets. Others feel stifled by them. Try both. Do you thrive on structure, or do you prefer freedom?

Keep a Process Journal:

Reflect on what works and what doesn't. Did you feel energized after a writing sprint? Or did slow, steady sessions feel more productive?

Write Without Rules (Just for Fun):

No plot, no outline, no expectations. Just write for the joy of it. See what happens when you let go of "shoulds" and "musts."

Staying Open to Growth

Here's the thing: what works for you now might change. And that's okay. Keep your mind open to new techniques, styles, and approaches. Your voice will evolve as you do.

Sometimes your muse will be loud and demanding; other times, you'll have to coax it out with snacks and motivational pep talks. Writing isn't about taming your muse--it's about learning to dance with it.

The Only Rule That Matters

Ready for it? The only rule of writing is: DO WHAT WORKS FOR YOU.

Not what works for your favorite author. Not what works for the guy with a million followers on Twitter. YOU.

Reflection Prompt:

What writing habits energize you? Which ones drain you? How can you create a process that feels authentic and sustainable for you?

Prayer:

God, thank You for the unique voice You've given me. Help me embrace my creative process with freedom and curiosity. Teach me to let go of comparison, trust my instincts, and find joy in the journey of writing. Amen.

CHAPTER 14:

THE FOUNDATION OF EVERYTHING -- MARKET RESEARCH FOR WRITERS

So, you've poured your heart into your writing, sculpted characters from the depths of your imagination, and crafted plots that could make even the most stoic reader gasp. But here's the kicker: if you want your words to reach beyond your laptop, you need to understand the foundation of marketing--and it all starts with market research.

Now, before you roll your eyes and think, "Ugh, marketing sounds like spreadsheets and corporate jargon," let me stop you right there. Marketing, at its core, is storytelling with a purpose. And guess what? You're already a storyteller.

Why Market Research Matters (Even If You Think It Doesn't)

Imagine throwing a message in a bottle into the ocean, hoping someone, somewhere, will find it. That's what marketing without research feels like. But what if you knew exactly where to throw that bottle to reach the right person at the right time? That's market research.

Market research helps you:

Understand your audience: Who are they? What do they love, hate, crave in a story?

Speak their language: Not just literally, but emotionally. What makes them click, buy, or binge-read?

Position your work: Knowing where your book fits helps you find your tribe--readers who will champion your work like it's the next big thing.

The Difference Between Writing and Selling (Hint: It's Not Selling Out)

Some writers think marketing means "selling out." Nope. It's about connection.

When you understand your audience, you're not shouting into the void. You're having a conversation. You're saying, "Hey, I see you. I wrote this for you." That's not selling out. That's being intentional.

Getting Started with Market Research (Without Losing Your Mind)

Define Your Ideal Reader:

Picture them. What books do they love? What keeps them up at night? What podcasts do they binge? The more specific, the better.

Stalk (In a Non-Creepy Way):

Check out Goodreads reviews of books similar to yours. What do readers rave about? What do they complain about?

Engage with Communities:

Join Facebook groups, subreddits, or online forums where your ideal readers hang out. Lurk, listen, and learn.

Survey Your Audience:

If you have an email list or social following, ask questions. What do they want more of? What do they struggle with?

Analyze Successful Authors:

Look at authors in your genre. What content do they post? How do they engage their audience?

Understanding Your Unique Voice in the Market

While research helps you find your audience, it should never dilute your unique voice. Think of it like cooking: knowing your guests' preferences helps you decide what to serve, but how you season it? That's all you.

Don't shape your writing to fit the market; find the readers who resonate with the stories you're already passionate about telling.

Faith, Authenticity, and Marketing

As a faith-driven writer, marketing might feel... weird. But here's the thing: authentic marketing is about serving, not selling.

Serve through your words: Your book might be the encouragement someone needs.

Serve through connection: Your authenticity can inspire more than your stories ever could.

Serve without fear: You were called to write. Don't be afraid to share that calling with others.

Reflection Prompt:

Who is your ideal reader? How can understanding them help you connect authentically without feeling like you're just "selling" your work?

Prayer:

God, thank You for the gift of words and the calling to share them. Help me approach marketing with authenticity, courage, and a heart for connection. Teach me to trust that my stories will reach those who need them most. Amen.

CHAPTER 15:

BUILDING YOUR AUTHOR BRAND WITHOUT LOSING YOUR SOUL

Let's face it: the term "author brand" sounds like something dreamed up in a corporate boardroom where people wear stiff suits and say things like, "Let's circle back." But here's the truth: your author brand isn't about logos or color schemes. It's about your authentic voice-- the one you've been honing through every word you write.

What Is an Author Brand (Really)?

Your brand is simply how people experience you as a writer. It's the feeling they get when they read your work, visit your website, or scroll through your social media. Think of it as the vibe you give off without even trying.

It's not about being fake or creating a polished persona. In fact, the best brands are rooted in authenticity. They reflect your values, your voice, and the unique stories only you can tell.

Why You Need an Author Brand (Even If You Cringe at the Thought)

It Creates Connection:

Readers don't just fall in love with books; they fall in love with authors. Your brand helps them feel like they know you, which keeps them coming back.

It Makes You Memorable:

There are millions of books out there. A strong brand helps you stand out in a crowded marketplace.

It Builds Trust:

Consistency in your voice and message helps readers know what to expect from you, whether it's cozy mysteries with a dash of humor or epic fantasies with deep emotional arcs.

How to Build Your Author Brand Without Feeling Like a Walking Billboard

Know Your "Why":

Why do you write? What do you hope your stories will do for readers? Your "why" is the heart of your brand.

Define Your Voice:

Are you snarky, poetic, heartfelt, or thought-provoking? Let that voice shine in everything you do--from your books to your blog posts to your Instagram captions.

Be Consistent, Not Robotic:

You don't need to sound the same in every post, but there should be a thread of authenticity that ties it all together.

Share the Person Behind the Words:

Readers love getting a glimpse of the real you. Share your writing process, your struggles, your triumphs... even your coffee addiction (if applicable).

Focus on Relationships, Not Just Reach:

Building a brand isn't about shouting into the void for followers. It's about connecting with people who resonate with your words.

The Faith Factor: Staying Grounded in Your Values

As a faith-driven writer, your brand isn't just a marketing tool-- it's an extension of your calling. It should reflect your values, not just your writing style.

Authenticity Over Perfection: You don't need to curate a flawless image. People connect with realness.

Service Over Self-Promotion: Approach your brand as a way to serve your audience, not just sell to them.

Courage Over Comparison: Don't measure your worth by likes, shares, or follower counts. Your value comes from who you are, not how many people click a button.

Practical Branding Tips (Without the Corporate Jargon)

Create a Simple Tagline: What's your writing all about? (Example: "Stories of hope, heart, and humor" or "Fiction with a faith-filled twist.")

Choose Visuals That Feel Like You: Pick colors, fonts, and images that reflect your vibe. (Think cozy and warm? Or bold and dramatic?)

Keep It Real: The best branding advice? Be yourself... but slightly more organized.

Reflection Prompt:

What do you want readers to feel when they engage with your work? How can you reflect that in your author brand?

Prayer:

God, thank You for the unique story You've written into my life. Help me share it authentically, with courage and grace. Teach me to build connections that reflect Your love and to trust that my words will reach those who need them most. Amen.

CHAPTER 16:

SOCIAL MEDIA FOR WRITERS -- MORE THAN JUST BOOK PROMO

Ah, social media. The place where memes thrive, cat videos rule, and everyone seems to have an opinion on everything from coffee preferences to the meaning of life. As a writer, it can feel overwhelming. Do you need to be everywhere? Do you have to post daily? And what on earth do you even say?

Here's the truth: Social media isn't just about promoting your book. It's about building connections, sharing your voice, and creating a space where readers feel like they know you. (Yes, even if you're an introvert.)

Why Social Media Matters (Even If You'd Rather Be Writing)

Connection Over Promotion:

People don't follow authors just to be sold to. They follow for the behind-the-scenes moments, the relatable struggles, the humor, and the heart.

Visibility:

Social media helps you reach new readers who might never stumble across your book in a bookstore.

Authenticity Shines:

You don't have to be flashy. You just have to be you. Readers connect with realness, not perfectly curated feeds.

Choosing the Right Platforms (Hint: You Don't Need Them All)

Focus on the platforms where your readers hang out and where you feel comfortable.

Instagram: Great for visuals, quotes, and aesthetic vibes.

Facebook: Ideal for groups and building community.

Twitter/X: Perfect for witty one-liners, quick thoughts, and engaging with writing communities.

TikTok: If you love short videos and creative storytelling.

Pinterest: Surprisingly powerful for blog posts, book aesthetics, and evergreen content.

Pick 1-2 platforms to start. Consistency matters more than quantity.

What to Post (Without Feeling Like a Sales Robot)

Your Writing Journey:

Share your process, struggles, victories, and the occasional "I stared at my screen for an hour and wrote one sentence" post. Relatable content wins.

Quotes and Excerpts:

Tease snippets from your work. Give readers a taste of your style.

Behind-the-Scenes:
Your messy desk, your writing playlist, your favorite mug. It's the little things that build connection.

Personal Stories:

You don't have to overshare, but letting readers see the person behind the pages makes your work more meaningful.

Encouragement and Inspiration:

Share what inspires you. Quotes, reflections, faith-driven messages--whatever aligns with your voice.

Engagement Over Perfection

You don't need to be a social media guru. Focus on engaging instead of performing.

Respond to Comments: Make people feel seen.

Ask Questions: Simple prompts can spark conversations. (Example: "What's your current favorite read?")

Be Consistent: You don't have to post daily, but showing up regularly builds connection.

The Faith Factor: Navigating Social Media with Purpose

Social media can be noisy. It's easy to get caught up in comparison, chasing likes, or feeling like you're shouting into the void. But as a faith-driven writer, you have a different perspective:

You're not here to impress. You're here to connect.

Your worth isn't tied to metrics. God's plan isn't based on algorithms.

Your words have purpose, even if they reach just one person.

Setting Boundaries (Because Burnout Isn't the Goal)

Schedule Your Posts: Batch content in advance to avoid daily stress.

Take Breaks: Digital detoxes are healthy. Your audience will understand.

Guard Your Heart: If scrolling makes you feel anxious, step back. Social media should be a tool, not a burden.

Reflection Prompt:

How can you use social media to authentically connect with readers without feeling overwhelmed?

Prayer:

God, thank You for the opportunity to connect with others through my words. Help me use social media with intention and authenticity. Teach me to find balance, to guard my heart, and to trust that even the smallest message can make a difference. Amen.

CHAPTER 17:

CONNECTING WITH READERS -- COMMUNITY OVER SALES

Let's be real: no one wakes up excited to be sold something. We're bombarded with ads everywhere--on our phones, in our inboxes, even while scrolling for cat memes. But you know what we do love? Authentic connection. And that's where writers have a secret superpower.

Your words don't just tell stories; they build bridges.

Why Connection Matters More Than Sales

People Buy from People They Trust:

Readers aren't just looking for books; they're looking for voices that resonate with them. Build trust first, and the sales will follow.

Long-Term Relationships > Quick Wins:

A viral post might get you temporary attention, but genuine connections create loyal readers who stick around for the long haul.

Your Story Is More Than Your Book:

Your personal journey, your creative process, your struggles--these are the stories that connect you with readers on a deeper level.

How to Build a Reader Community (Without Feeling Like a Pushy Salesperson)

Engage Authentically:

Comment on posts, reply to messages, and be genuinely interested. Think of social media as a conversation, not a megaphone.

Share Your Journey:

Readers love seeing the person behind the pages. Talk about your writing process, the challenges you face, and the small wins along the way.

Ask Questions:

People love to share their opinions. Ask about their favorite books, characters, or writing tips. It's a simple way to spark conversations.

Create Value:

Offer more than just "buy my book" posts. Share writing tips, book recommendations, inspiring quotes, or even funny stories from your writing life.

Be Consistent:

You don't have to post every day, but showing up regularly keeps the connection alive.

Faith-Driven Connection: Leading with Purpose

As faith-driven writers, we have the unique opportunity to connect on a soul level, not just a surface one.

Be a Light: Share messages of hope, encouragement, and authenticity.

Lead with Service: Approach your platform with the heart to serve, not just promote.

Trust the Impact: You may never know how deeply your words touch someone. Trust that every authentic connection matters.

Practical Ways to Nurture Your Reader Community

Start a Newsletter: It's more personal than social media and goes directly to your readers' inboxes.

Host Q&A Sessions: Go live on social media or host virtual meetups where readers can ask questions and connect with you.

Create Reader Groups: Consider a private Facebook group where your biggest fans can engage with you and each other.

Highlight Your Readers: Share fan art, reviews, or testimonials to celebrate the people who support your work.

The Balance Between Personal and Professional

You don't have to share every detail of your life. Boundaries are healthy. Decide what feels authentic to share and what you prefer to keep private. Connection doesn't require oversharing--just sincerity.

Reflection Prompt:

How can you create meaningful connections with your readers that go beyond just selling your books?

Prayer:

God, thank You for the gift of community. Help me connect with my readers authentically, to encourage and inspire through my words. Teach me to value relationships over results, and to trust that every connection serves a greater purpose. Amen.

CHAPTER 18:

THE BALANCE OF CREATIVITY AND MARKETING

Ah, the eternal struggle: how do you keep your creative spark alive while also juggling the demands of marketing your work? It's like trying to ride two horses at once--one named "Inspiration" and the other named "Obligation." Spoiler alert: it's possible, but it requires balance, intentionality, and maybe a little bit of grace (okay, a lot).

The Creative vs. Marketing Tug-of-War

The Creative Flow:

Writing is your heart space. It's where you feel alive, where ideas bloom, and where you get lost in the rhythm of words.

The Marketing Hustle:

Marketing is strategic. It's about showing up consistently, promoting your work, and engaging with your audience.

The challenge? Marketing can feel like it drains your creative energy, while creativity can make marketing feel like an afterthought.

Finding Harmony (Not Just Balance)

Balance implies an equal split, but harmony is about blending the two in a way that feels natural. Think of it like a well-crafted novel: the plot (marketing) drives the story, but the characters (creativity) give it heart.

Strategies to Keep Both Horses Moving

Batch Your Marketing Tasks:

Set aside specific days or hours for marketing. Create content in batches so you can focus on writing the rest of the time.

Incorporate Creativity into Marketing:

Think of marketing as storytelling. Share behind-the-scenes moments, character insights, or the inspiration behind your work. Make it fun, not a chore.

Set Clear Boundaries:

Protect your creative time fiercely. Turn off notifications, set timers, and create a routine that prioritizes your writing.

Align Your Content with Your Passion:

If you love writing about certain topics, infuse that into your marketing. Authenticity resonates more than polished perfection.

Automate Where You Can:

Use tools to schedule posts, manage emails, and streamline tasks so you can spend more time in your creative zone.

The Faith Factor: Trusting the Process

As faith-driven writers, it's easy to feel overwhelmed by the pressure to "do it all." But here's the truth: you don't have to hustle your way into purpose.

Pray Over Your Work: Both the creative and the marketing sides. Ask for guidance, clarity, and inspiration.

Release the Outcome: Do your part, but trust God with the results.

Serve, Don't Strive: Shift your mindset from "how can I sell more books?" to "how can I serve my readers with my words?"

Practical Tips to Stay Grounded

Morning Rituals: Start your day with prayer, reflection, or journaling to center your mind.

Creative Breaks: When marketing feels overwhelming, step back. Write something just for fun--no agenda, no deadlines.

Celebrate Small Wins: Every connection, every post, every page written is progress. Acknowledge it.

Reflection Prompt:

How can you integrate your creative passion with your marketing efforts in a way that feels authentic and life-giving?

Prayer:

God, thank You for the gift of creativity and the opportunities to share my work. Help me find harmony between my passion for writing and the tasks of marketing. Teach me to trust the process, to rest in Your timing, and to serve with a heart full of purpose. Amen.

CHAPTER 19:

WRITING WITH GOD -- THE HEARTBEAT OF YOUR CREATIVE JOURNEY

When people talk about "writing with God," it often conjures up images of a shining light descending on your laptop, your fingers flying over the keys as divine inspiration flows effortlessly through you. Spoiler alert: it doesn't work like that. Writing with God isn't a mystical experience reserved for a chosen few. It's not about waiting for some magical burst of inspiration where the heavens open and your manuscript writes itself.

Jesus was a carpenter. Think about that for a second. He worked with His hands, shaping wood into something both useful and beautiful. Writing with God is much the same. It's about showing up, doing the work, and trusting that in the process, something sacred can emerge--not because it's perfect, but because it's offered with intention.

What Writing with God Really Means

Writing with God is less about what you write and more about why you write. It's about creating with purpose, rooted in the understanding that your words have the potential to reflect His light--whether you're writing devotionals, fiction, poetry, or even social media posts.

Intention Over Perfection:

Writing with God isn't about producing flawless work. It's about setting an intention: How can my words serve? Who am I writing for? It's the willingness to show up, even when the words don't flow easily, trusting that the act of writing itself holds value.

Surrendering the Outcome:

When you write with God, you're not responsible for controlling the impact of your words. Your job is to write; God handles the rest. Maybe your words will reach thousands, or maybe they'll touch just one heart. Both are sacred.

Revealing, Not Preaching:

Writing in faith isn't about sounding holy or delivering sermons disguised as stories. It's about revealing glimpses of grace, hope, and truth through authentic storytelling. Sometimes God speaks the loudest through the quietest moments in your prose.

Creating Space for His Voice:

Writing with God means leaving room for reflection. Not every moment needs to be filled with action or clever dialogue.

Sometimes, it's in the pauses--the white space between the words--where His presence feels the strongest.

The Practical Side of Writing with God

Let's ditch the idea that writing with God requires a specific ritual or perfect conditions. Here's what it really looks like:

Pray Before You Write: Not for perfection, but for clarity and openness.

Invite God Into the Process: Whether you're brainstorming, stuck on a scene, or editing for the tenth time, whisper, "God, guide me."

Write with an Open Heart: Let go of the pressure to impress. Focus on expressing, not performing.

What Writing with God Is Not

It's Not Easy: Just because you're writing with God doesn't mean the words will flow effortlessly. You'll still face writer's block, doubt, and frustration.

It's Not About Fame: Writing with God isn't a shortcut to success. It's about faithfulness, not followers.

It's Not Reserved for "Christian" Content: You don't have to write overtly spiritual stories for your work to be infused with divine purpose. God shows up in every genre, every style.

The Power of Intention

When you write with God, you're not just putting words on a page. You're creating with intention, reflecting the beauty, complexity, and hope woven into the human experience. Your words become more than just sentences; they become seeds planted in the hearts of readers.

Practical Resources for Writing with God

Here are some exercises and activities to help you engage more deeply with your faith-driven writing practice:

Prayer Journaling:

Before each writing session, spend 5-10 minutes journaling a prayer. Ask for guidance, clarity, and inspiration. Reflect on what comes up, and let it inform your writing.

Scripture Prompts:

Choose a verse and write a short reflection or story inspired by it. How does it speak to your current writing project or creative process?

Gratitude Lists:

List five things you're grateful for related to your writing journey. This practice keeps you grounded and fosters a positive mindset, even on tough writing days.

Write a Letter to God:

Pour out your thoughts, frustrations, and hopes in the form of a letter to God. It's a powerful way to process emotions and find clarity.

Creative Worship:

Write a poem, song, or story purely as an act of worship. No agenda, no audience--just you and God.

Reflection Prompts:

Where do I feel God's presence most strongly in my writing?

How do my stories reflect the values and truths I hold dear?

What does it mean for me to surrender my writing to God?

Reflection Prompt:

How do you invite God into your writing process? What shifts when you focus less on the outcome and more on the intention behind your words?

Prayer:

God, thank You for the gift of words and the privilege of storytelling. Help me to write with purpose, to create with intention, and to trust You with the process and the outcome. May my words reflect Your light, even in the smallest ways. Use my writing to touch hearts, bring hope, and reveal Your presence. Amen.

EXTRAS

Pop Culture Quiz: Which Famous Writer Shares Your Writing Style?

Answer these quick questions to find your literary spirit twin:

What's your ideal writing environment?

    A) A cozy corner with endless coffee.
    B) A cabin in the woods, complete solitude.
    C) A bustling café with background chatter.
    D) Late at night when the world is asleep.

What's your biggest writing challenge?

    A) Getting started.
    B) Staying focused.
    C) Over-editing.
    D) Finishing what I start.

Your writing voice feels most like:

    A) Poetic and reflective.
    B) Dark and introspective.
    C) Witty and conversational.
    D) Bold and dramatic.

Results:

Mostly A's: Jane Austen vibes -- Thoughtful, observant, with sharp insights on life and relationships.

Mostly B's: C.S. Lewis energy -- Deep, philosophical, with a strong faith thread.

Mostly C's: Anne Lamott style -- Honest, raw, and relatable with a dash of humor.

Mostly D's: J.K. Rowling flair -- Imaginative, detailed, and rich with storytelling magic.

Reflection Prompt:

How do you invite God into your writing process? What shifts when you focus less on the outcome and more on the intention behind your words?

Prayer:

God, thank You for the gift of words and the privilege of storytelling. Help me to write with purpose, to create with intention, and to trust You with the process and the outcome. May my words reflect Your light, even in the smallest ways. Use my writing to touch hearts, bring hope, and reveal Your presence. Amen

Quizzes & Resources: Tools for Writers

Welcome to the fun zone! This section is packed with interactive quizzes, practical tools, and exercises designed to help you overcome common writing challenges, spark creativity, and discover more about your unique writing process. Whether you're stuck on a scene, battling writer's block, or just need a little inspiration, this section is here to guide you.

Pop Culture Quiz 1: Which Fictional Character Would Be Your Writing Buddy?

What motivates you to write?

- A) Adventure and new ideas.
- B) Deep emotional expression.
- C) A desire to change the world.
- D) The thrill of mystery and suspense.

Your ideal writing environment is:

- A) A cozy nook with a view of nature.
- B) A bustling café with ambient noise.
- C) A minimalist space with zero distractions.
- D) Late-night sessions with moody lighting.

What's your biggest writing challenge?

- A) Staying focused.
- B) Overthinking every word.
- C) Starting new projects.
- D) Finishing what you start.

Results:

Mostly A's: Anne Shirley from Anne of Green Gables - Whimsical, imaginative, and bursting with creativity.

Mostly B's: Elizabeth Bennet from Pride and Prejudice - Sharp, witty, and emotionally intelligent.

Mostly C's: Atticus Finch from To Kill a Mockingbird - Thoughtful, principled, and driven by purpose.

Mostly D's: Sherlock Holmes from Sherlock Holmes - Analytical, detail-oriented, and always chasing the next puzzle.

Quiz 2: Are You a Pantser or a Plotter?

How do you start a new story?

    A) With a detailed outline, knowing exactly where it's going.
    B) I dive right in and see where the characters take me.

When writing, do you prefer:

    A) Structure and clear milestones to guide me.
    B) The freedom to explore without constraints.

How do you handle plot twists?

    A) I plan them carefully in advance.
    B) They surprise me as much as they surprise my characters.

What happens if you get stuck?

    A) I refer back to my outline for direction.
    B) I let the story sit until inspiration strikes again.

Your writing process feels like:

    A) Building a puzzle with all the pieces in place.
    B) Going on an adventure with no map.

Results:

Mostly A's: Plotter - You love structure, organization, and knowing where your story is headed.

Mostly B's: Pantser - You thrive on creative freedom, discovering the story as you go.

A Mix: Plantser - A delightful hybrid, blending loose planning with spontaneous creativity.

Quiz 3: What Genre Writer Are You?

What type of stories do you gravitate towards?

    A) Epic adventures with complex worlds.
    B) Heartfelt dramas with deep emotional connections.
    C) Fast-paced thrillers with lots of twists.
    D) Lighthearted tales filled with humor and charm.

Your ideal protagonist is:

    A) A brave hero on a grand quest.
    B) A flawed character searching for meaning.
    C) A detective unraveling a dark mystery.
    D) A quirky underdog navigating everyday life.

What keeps your readers hooked?

    A) Intricate world-building and lore.
    B) Emotional depth and character growth.
    C) Suspense and unexpected plot twists.
    D) Relatable humor and witty dialogue.

Your writing style is:

    A) Descriptive and immersive.
    B) Poetic and introspective.
    C) Sharp and action-packed.
    D) Fun, light, and entertaining.

Results:

Mostly A's: Fantasy/Sci-Fi Writer - You love creating new worlds filled with magic, adventure, or futuristic tech.

Mostly B's: Literary/Contemporary Writer - Your stories explore deep emotions, relationships, and personal growth.

Mostly C's: Mystery/Thriller Writer - You thrive on suspense, intrigue, and keeping readers on the edge of their seats.

Mostly D's: Rom-Com/Light Fiction Writer - Your stories are charming, funny, and perfect for readers who love a good laugh with heart.

Writer's Block Toolkit: Quick Fixes for When You're Stuck

The 10-Minute Rule: Set a timer for 10 minutes and write without stopping. No edits, no judgment--just words.

Change Your Scenery: Write in a different location. A new environment can spark fresh ideas.

Dialogue Sprint: Write a conversation between two characters. No descriptions, just pure dialogue.

Switch Mediums: Try handwriting instead of typing, or use a voice recorder to speak your ideas out loud.

Write the Worst Sentence: Challenge yourself to write the worst opening line possible. It's freeing, and often leads to unexpected inspiration.

Self-Editing Checklist: Polish Like a Pro

Clarity: Does each sentence convey its meaning clearly?

Consistency: Are character behaviors, timelines, and details consistent?

Pacing: Does the story flow smoothly, with a balance of action and reflection?

Dialogue: Does the dialogue sound natural and true to each character?

Word Choice: Are you using strong, specific language?

Show, Don't Tell: Are you painting vivid scenes rather than just stating facts?

Grammar & Spelling: Run spellcheck, but also read aloud to catch errors.

Productivity Hacks for Writers

Pomodoro Technique: Write for 25 minutes, then take a 5-minute break. Repeat.

Word Sprints: Set a word count goal (e.g., 500 words) and race against the clock.

Accountability Buddy: Partner with another writer to share goals and check in regularly.

Reward System: Set small rewards for hitting milestones (like a favorite snack or a mini break).

Theme Days: Dedicate specific days to different tasks (e.g., Monday = drafting, Wednesday = editing).

Reflection Prompts for Ongoing Growth

What inspires me to write, even on difficult days?

How do I handle creative setbacks, and what helps me bounce back?

What unique perspective do I bring to my stories?

How does my faith influence my writing process?

What are three things I've learned about myself through writing?

Prayer for Writers:

God, thank You for the gift of creativity and the courage to share my words. When I feel stuck, remind me that inspiration comes in many forms. Help me to write with honesty, passion, and faith, trusting that my words will find their purpose. Amen.

Christian Writing Prompts: From Easy to Challenging

Welcome to your creative playground! This section is designed to spark inspiration, deepen your faith, and stretch your storytelling skills. Whether you're new to writing or a seasoned author, these prompts will guide you through different genres and themes, from simple reflections to complex narratives.

Easy Prompts (Warm-Up Your Creativity)

Personal Reflection:

Write about a time you felt God's presence in an unexpected place. How did it change your perspective?

Faith in a Sentence:

Describe your faith journey in just one sentence. Now expand that sentence into a paragraph, then into a full page.

Modern Psalm:

Write your own Psalm inspired by David's style. Express gratitude, struggles, and praise in your unique voice.

Intermediate Prompts (Stretch Your Storytelling Muscles)

The Parable Twist:

Take a well-known parable from the Bible and rewrite it in a modern setting. How would the Good Samaritan story unfold in today's world?

Letters to God:

Write a letter from the perspective of a biblical character (like Mary, Peter, or Jonah) reflecting on a pivotal moment in their life.

Faith Meets Fiction:

Create a fictional character who is struggling with their faith. Write a scene where they encounter someone or something that challenges their beliefs.

Advanced Prompts (Deep Dive into Complex Themes)

The Silent Gospel:

Write a story where none of the characters explicitly mention God or faith, yet the theme of redemption is unmistakably woven throughout.

Alternate Timeline:

Imagine a world where a major biblical event never happened (e.g., the flood, the Exodus, or Pentecost). How would history have unfolded differently? Explore the ripple effects in a short story.

The Prayer That Changed Everything:

Write a story centered around a single prayer--it could be whispered in desperation, shouted in anger, or quietly hopeful. Show how this prayer transforms the character's life in unexpected ways.

Bonus Challenge: Faith-Fueled Flash Fiction

Write a complete story in 300 words or less that explores the theme of hope, forgiveness, or grace. Every word counts, so focus on powerful imagery and emotional impact.

Reflection Questions:

Which prompt challenged you the most, and why?

How did your faith influence the way you approached these stories?

What did you discover about your writing style through these exercises?

Prayer for Inspiration:

God, thank You for the gift of words and the courage to share stories that reflect Your love and truth. Bless my creativity, guide my heart, and help me write with purpose and authenticity. May my words inspire, heal, and draw others closer to You. Amen.

Christian Writing Prompts for a Secular Reading World

These prompts challenge you to weave faith-based themes into stories that resonate with a broader audience, without overt religious language. The goal is to reflect God's truth through universal experiences of love, loss, hope, and redemption.

The Invisible Anchor:

Write a story about a character who faces overwhelming odds but finds unexplainable peace and strength from within. How do they navigate their struggles, and what unseen force guides them?

The Light They Can't Explain:

Create a character who encounters an extraordinary act of kindness or grace that defies logic. How does this event ripple through their life and the lives of others?

The Choice:

Write about a pivotal moment where a character must choose between revenge and forgiveness. Explore the emotional tension and the consequences of their decision without explicitly mentioning faith or morality.

Reflection Questions:

Which prompt challenged you the most, and why?

How did your faith influence the way you approached these stories?

What did you discover about your writing style through these exercises?

Prayer for Inspiration:

God, thank You for the gift of words and the courage to share stories that reflect Your love and truth. Bless my creativity, guide my heart, and help me write with purpose and authenticity. May my words inspire, heal, and draw others closer to You. Amen.

Advice for the Novice Writer Who Feels Lost

If you're new to writing and feeling overwhelmed, unsure where to start, or drowning in self-doubt, you're not alone. Every writer--yes, even the greats--has been where you are. The good news? You don't have to figure it all out at once.

Start with What You Love

Pick a book, film, or TV show that you absolutely adore in the genre you want to write. Don't just watch or read it passively--study it. This isn't cheating; it's learning the craft.

Reverse Outline:

Break Down Each Scene:

Identify what happens in each scene. Ask yourself:

What is the conflict here?

What drives the characters' decisions?

How does this scene move the story forward?

Analyze the Dialogue:

Study how characters talk to each other. Notice how dialogue reveals personality, builds tension, or conveys subtext without saying things outright.

Find the Emotional Core:

Every great story has an emotional heartbeat. Pinpoint what pulls at your heartstrings and ask why it works.

Make It Your Own

Once you have a basic outline, don't be afraid to tweak it. Change the characters, the setting, the stakes--whatever sparks your imagination. This isn't about copying; it's about understanding story mechanics.

Why This Isn't Cheating

Here's the secret: every story has been told. But it hasn't been told by you. Your voice, your perspective, your heart--that's what makes it original.

So take that outline, mold it into something new, and start writing. Go through the process. Learn, fail, get frustrated, celebrate small wins... and then keep going. Writing isn't about getting it perfect; it's about showing up.

Reflection Questions:

What story inspired you to start writing in the first place?

How can studying your favorite stories help you grow as a writer?

What is the unique message only you can share through your writing?

Prayer for New Writers:

God, thank You for planting the seed of creativity in my heart. When I feel lost, remind me that every step I take, even the messy ones, is part of the journey. Help me to trust the process, to find my voice, and to write with courage and authenticity. Amen.

For the Writer with 100,000 Words and No Clear Focus

Maybe you're not lost at the starting line--maybe you're buried under a mountain of words, unsure of what your book is even about anymore. You can't summarize your story without a slideshow, a flowchart, and maybe interpretive dance. Don't worry. You're not alone.

How This Book Can Help:

Find the Core Conflict:

Go back to basics. What is your protagonist's goal? What stands in their way? If you can identify the central conflict, you've found the heart of your story.

Reverse Outline Your Own Work:

Just like studying a favorite book or film, break down your manuscript scene by scene:

What happens in each scene?

Does it move the plot forward or develop the characters?

If it doesn't serve a purpose, consider cutting or revising it.

Write the One-Sentence Summary:

Challenge yourself to describe your book in one sentence. If that's hard, great! It means you're digging into the core of your story. Refine it until it clicks.

It's Not Cheating to Simplify:

Complexity is great, but clarity is essential. Simplifying your story doesn't make it shallow; it makes it readable.

Encouragement for the Overwhelmed Writer:

You don't have to untangle the entire mess at once. Take it one scene, one sentence, one character at a time. Your story matters. It just needs a little refining to let it shine.

Reflection Questions:

What is the heartbeat of my story?

Which scenes are my favorites, and why? Do they reflect my core theme?

If I had to pitch my book in one sentence, what would I say?

Prayer for Clarity:

God, thank You for the gift of creativity and the courage to tell stories. When I feel lost in my own words, guide me back to the heart of my story. Help me to see with fresh eyes, to edit with purpose, and to trust that the story You placed in my heart is worth sharing. Amen.

Prayers for Writers

As you continue your writing journey, here are prayers to inspire, comfort, and guide you through the creative process. Whether you're facing writer's block, seeking clarity, or celebrating a breakthrough, let these words be a reminder that God is with you in every step of your writing journey.

Prayer for Creative Inspiration:

God, You are the ultimate Creator. Inspire my heart and mind with fresh ideas. Help me see beauty in the ordinary and find words that reflect Your truth. May my creativity be a reflection of Your boundless imagination. Amen.

Prayer for Overcoming Writer's Block:

Lord, when my words feel stuck and my thoughts are clouded, clear my mind and calm my spirit. Help me release perfectionism and write with freedom. Remind me that even in the silence, You are present. Amen.

Prayer for Clarity and Focus:

Father, grant me clarity as I write. Help me focus on the message You want me to share. Remove distractions and doubts, and guide my words to be meaningful and authentic. Amen.

Prayer for Courage to Share My Work:

God, give me the courage to share my words, even when I feel vulnerable. Help me trust that my voice matters and that my story can impact others. Let me write not for approval, but to honor the gift You've given me. Amen.

Prayer for Finding My Unique Voice:

Lord, help me embrace the writer You created me to be. Let me write with honesty, boldness, and authenticity. May my unique voice reflect Your love and light in ways only I can express. Amen.

Prayer for Perseverance:

Dear God, writing can be hard. When I feel discouraged or overwhelmed, remind me why I started. Fill me with perseverance, discipline, and the determination to keep going. Amen.

Prayer of Gratitude for the Gift of Writing:

Thank You, God, for the gift of words. Thank You for the ability to create, imagine, and inspire through storytelling. May I never take this gift for granted. Use my writing to bring hope, encouragement, and truth to those who need it. Amen.

Prayer for Writers Facing Doubt:

Heavenly Father, doubt creeps in when I least expect it. Remind me that my worth is not tied to my words, and my identity is found in You. Strengthen my confidence and help me write with faith, not fear. Amen.

Prayer for Rest and Renewal:

Lord, when I feel drained and creatively empty, help me find rest in You. Renew my spirit, refresh my mind, and restore my passion for writing. Remind me that rest is part of the process. Amen.

Final Blessing for Writers:

May your words be filled with purpose, your stories woven with truth, and your heart always open to the whisper of God. Keep writing, keep believing, and trust that your words matter because they come from the One who speaks life into us all. Amen.

Made in the USA
Coppell, TX
19 April 2025

48440150R00066